January 18, 1995 —

To: Dr. Nancy Wexler
Dr. Herbert Pardes —

With admiration
and respect —

Dr. Samuel I & Ethel LeFrak

Andy Warhol, (American, 1928-1987), **Sam and Ethel LeFrak,** 1982, Oil and silkscreen on canvas, 40 x 40 inches (102 x 102 cms.)

MASTERS
OF
THE MODERN TRADITION

Selections from
The Collection of Samuel J. and Ethel LeFrak

Catalogue by
Diane Kelder
Professor of Art History
City University of New York

INDEX OF ARTISTS AND WORKS

FOREWORD

More than a hundred years ago, a group of remarkable painters introduced one of the most exciting bodies of work in the history of art. Breaking free from the constraints and prejudices imposed by the official art establishment, they revolutionized concepts of painting that would affect it as no other movement before or since. Rejecting traditional subject matter and slick academic technique, these mavericks immersed themselves in the visual experience of the present and sought new expressive means through which to capture the unique, fleeting reality of the moment. Leaving their studios, they set up their easels in suburban gardens, in country fields, on beaches, above crowded boulevards—even amidst the bustle of large railroad stations.

Initially, their efforts were met with skepticism and derision from both critics and the general public. Yet in less than a decade, they changed forever the way in which paintings were conceived, executed, and exhibited. Liberating line and color from their traditional functions of modeling and describing forms, Monet, Renoir, Degas, Pissarro, Cézanne and others set in motion an aesthetic revolution which gained momentum in the last years of the nineteenth century and led to the birth of abstract art in the twentieth.

The achievements of these original Impressionists were indispensable to the artistic development of Van Gogh, Gauguin, Bonnard and Vuillard. Moreover, they played an equally vital part in the growth of the founders of Modernism— Picasso, Matisse, and Kandinsky—who ultimately went far beyond inherited assumptions of what a painting could or should be.

Sharing a common bond of courage and a commitment to freedom and innovation, their belief in the future of painting was expressed in the radically new visual language that they were creating.

Their outstanding legacy and enduring appeal comes from the palpable sense of freshness and energy in their canvases which attest to their profound connection with life and also stimulate us to experience vicariously their very process of creation.

It has been our distinct pride and pleasure to have spent more than forty years collecting the work of Impressionist, Post-Impressionist, and other modern masters of the past hundred years. By their presence in our office and home, we often have been inspired to emulate their lifelong example of breaking old molds and of creating new standards for others to use.

As challenging and fascinating as collecting has been for us, it represents but one part of a lifelong interest in the arts. Patronage of individual artists as well as support for institutions that provide a forum for exhibitions and for the performing arts have been responsibilities we have gladly assumed for we see art in all its forms as man's most expressive affirmation of life. And we view collecting— like building—as but another manifestation of one's faith in the future.

The wish to share our collection with friends, with scholars, and students has been of vital concern to us. For more than twenty-five years, we have created and mailed holiday cards reproducing works in the collection. Each card has also expressed our thoughts and appreciation of the painting and its paean to life.

The publication of this book—illustrating and documenting a substantial part of our collection—has been undertaken in this spirit of sharing and in the hope that it will afford readers the boundless pleasure and inspiration we have discovered in and through art.

Samuel J. and Ethel LeFrak
New York, May, 1988

Eugène Delacroix
(French, 1798-1863)

La Juive D'Alger,
c. 1833?
Signed Eugène Delacroix in upper right
Oil on canvas
18 1/2 x 15 1/2 inches (47 x 39.5 cms.)

Provenance
Mrs. Lloyd Bruce Wescott, Clinton, New Jersey; Alex Reid &
Lefevre Ltd., (c. 1944), London; Paul Rosenberg & Co., New
York; E.V.Thaw & Co., Inc., New York; Norton Simon,
Fullerton, California (1964-71); Park-Bernet, New York, Sale
3202, May 5, 1971, lot 4.

Exhibitions
New York, Wildenstein Gallery, *Delacroix*, October 18-
November 18, 1944, no. 7, illustrated in catalogue; London,
Lefevre Galleries, *XIX and XX Century Paintings*, 1956, no. 8,
illustrated in catalogue.

Literature
Alfred Robaut, *L'Oeuvre complet de Eugène Delacroix*, Paris,
1885, no. 461; Lee Johnson, *The Paintings of Eugène Delacroix,
A Critical Catalogue*, Oxford, 1986, Vol. III, No. 388, ill. pl. 196

Delacroix's interest in exotic subjects was well established before the French conquest of Algeria in 1831. An invitation to participate in a government-sponsored mission to neighboring Morocco provided the opportunity to develop a wider range of exotic motifs. He arrived in Tangiers on January 26, 1832. Later that month, he wrote his friend Pierret, expressing his admiration for the beautiful Jewish women he had seen and indicating his intention of painting them:

"Les juives sont admirables, je crains qu'il ne soit difficile d'en faire autre chose que de les peindres: ce sont des perles d'Eden." (Correspondance. t, I., p.174)

Lee Johnson has tentatively dated this canvas 1852 on the basis of its correspondence to a painting titled *Une Juive chez-elle avec une femme mauresque* which was exhibited that year by the *Société des Amis des Arts* of Bordeaux (no.134). He theorizes that it was purchased from the exhibition by T.B.G. Scott, the Vice-President of the Société, and that it was shown again in an exhibition in Bordeaux that followed the painter's death in 1864.

A picture of this description was bought by Goupil and Company in February, 1874 and sold to the dealer, Georges Petit. So far it has not been possible to determine its whereabouts between that date and its acquisition by Mrs. Lloyd Bruce Westcott.

Johnson assumes that this painting and another variation of the subject (Johnson, no.389), which was purchased by Walter P. Chrysler in 1960 and sold to Masoud Rejaee in 1976, are dependent on the etching by Delacroix, *Une Juive d'Alger* (Robaut, no. 461) dated 1833. He argues that this painting is the earlier of the two versions since it conforms more closely, albeit in reverse, to the compositional details of the etching.

14

La Juive D'Alger, *(detail)*

Honoré Daumier
(French, 1808-1879)

Le Médecin Diafoirus (Une Tête de Médecin de Moliere)
c. 1870
Signed h. Daumier lower right
Oil on panel
8 7/8 x 6 3/4 inches (22.5 x 17.2 cms.)

Provenance
Aubry (Purchased from the artist April 20, 1877); Sale, Paris, 1897, no. 4; Hazard, Sale, Paris, 1919, no.4; Orrouy, Paris; François, Sale, Paris, 1935, no. 1; Galerie M. Bernheim, Paris; Galerie Thannhauser, Lucerne; (?) Rosengart, Switzerland, 1937; Dr. Ruth Morris Bakwin, New York; Sotheby's, New York, Sale, *Impressionist and Modern Paintings and Sculpture*, Part I, November 13, 1985, lot. 33.

Exhibitions
Paris, Galerie Durand-Ruel, *Exposition des Peintures et Dessins de Honoré Daumier*, 1878, no.6; (?) Paris, Ecole des Beaux-Arts, *Daumier*, 1897, no. 1; Paris, Ecole des Beaux-Arts, *Expositions Daumier*, 1901, no. 470; Philadelphia, Pennsylvania Museum of Art, *Daumier* 1937; London, The Arts Council of Great Britain, Tate Gallery, *Daumier, Paintings and Drawings*,1961, no.60, (1865-68), illustrated in catalogue; New York, Wildenstein and Co., *The Doctor and Mrs. Harry Bakwin Collection*, 1967, no. 12, illustrated in catalogue; Wellesley, Massachusetts, Wellesley College, Jewett Art Center, *Nineteenth and Twentieth Century Paintings in the Collection of Dr. and Mrs. Harry Bakwin*, 1967

Literature
Eduard Fuchs, *Catalogue Raisonné de Daumier*, Paris, 1878 (as *Dr. Diafoirus, figure de Moliere*) no. 17a; Arsène Alexandre, *Honoré Daumier—L'Homme et l'oeuvre*, Paris, 1888, p.373; Eric Klossowski, *Honoré Daumier*,Munich, 1923, 65, p.91; Edward Fuchs, *Der Maler Daumier*, Munich, 1930, no. 17a, ill. p.46; J. Cherpin, in *Marseilles, Revue municipale*, vol.III, no. 29, 1956, pp. 41-42 (listed as missing); "Scapin and Geronte", in *Burlington Magazine*, October 1966; K.E. Maison, *Honoré Daumier, Catalogue Raisonné of the Paintings, Watercolors and Drawings*, New York 1968, vol. I, no I-223, pp. 173-174, ill. pl. 141 (circa 1870); Luigi Barzini, *l'Opera pittorica completa di Daumier*, Milan, 1971, no.283, ill. p.112

This small oil is Daumier's last representation of the pretentious quack physician in Moliers's comedy *le Malade Imaginaire*. The work is related to two earlier depictions, *le Malade Imaginaire* (1860-63) an oil study in the Barnes Collection, Merion, Pennsylvania, and an eponymous painting in the Philadelphia Museum of Art of the same period which depicts the doctor and his comic assistant attending the patently apprehensive patient. Both the Philadelphia painting and this canvas were included in Durand-Ruel's 1878 exhibition of drawings and paintings by Daumier.

Honoré Daumier

Avant L'Audience (Une Cause Criminelle) (Plaideur et Avocat)
c. 1855
Signed with initials h.d. in left corner
India ink, charcoal, and light wash on paper
8 3/4 x 9 inches (21 x 22.6 cms.)

Provenance
Eisenloeffel, Amsterdam; Galerie B.Houthakker, Amsterdam;
H.E. Ten Cate, Esq., Almelo; C.G. Boerner, Dusseldorf; Kornfeld
& Klipstein, Bern, June 17, 1965, no. 188; E.J. Van Wisselingh &
Co., Amsterdam; Norton Simon, Fullerton, California; Sotheby
Parke-Bernet, New York, Sale, May 2, 1973, no. 1

Exhibitions
Amsterdam, Galerie B. Houthakker, *Dessins Anciens,*1952, no.
16; Almelo, *Van Daumier tot Picasso,* 1956, no.30; Dusseldorf,
C.G. Boerner, *Weihnachtsausstellung,* 1964, no. 138

Literature
Fuchs, supplement, no. 318b., p. 64, ill., pl. 318; Dr. D.
Hannema, *Catalogue of the H.E. Ten Cate Collection,*
Rotterdam, 1955, no. 141, ill., pl. 132; Maison, 1968, vol. II, no.
652, p. 216, ill., pl. 247

As a child of ten, Daumier began earning his living as a
lawyer's messenger, serving writs on shopkeepers and artisans.
He developed a stock of models and a repertory of situations that
served him throughout his life and also provided the point of
departure for the satirical lithographs published in *La
Caricature* and *Le Charivari.*
This drawing is related to a watercolor *Le Defenseur*
(Maison, no. 653) in a private collection, Paris, and to the
drawing *Une cause criminelle* (Maison, no. 654) in the Victoria
and Albert Museum, London.

Johann Barthold Jongkind
(Dutch, 1819-1891)

Inland Canal
1866
Signed Jongkind and dated lower left
Oil on canvas
20 x 13 inches (50.8 x 33 cms.)

Provenance
Mrs. Henry Butler, Youngstown, Ohio; Butler Institute of Art, Youngstown, Ohio; Kennedy Galleries, New York 1970

Literature
Victorine Hefting, *Jongkind, sa vie, son oeuvre, son epoque*, Paris, 1975, no 370 *(Paysage hollandais)*, ill. p. 173

In the early 1860s, the Dutch painter spent considerable time in France, visiting the Normandy and Brittany coasts for painting expeditions and working extensively in the vicinity of Paris. 1866 was an especially productive year; the artist worked in Paris from May through August, and subsequently made his way via Belgium to Holland, where he remained for more than a month. From his correspondence we learn that Jongkind did a great many landscapes during that period and this canal view probably dates from September or October.

Unlike the Impressionists who painted out of doors, Jongkind's initial response to a motif took the form of a drawing or watercolor which he later reworked in oil in his studio

Pierre-Auguste Renoir
(French, 1841-1919)

Jardin des Tuileries
c. 1875-76
Signed Renoir lower right
Oil on canvas
8 1/2 x 11 1/2 inches (21.5 x 29.2 cms.)

22

Provenance
Bernard Dorival, Paris; Thorsten Laurins, Stockholm; Wildenstein & Co., Inc., New York; The Grover A. and Jeanne J. Magnin Collection, San Francisco; Parke-Bernet, New York, Sale 2907, October 15, 1969, lot 7.

Exhibitions
Stockholm, National Museum, *Foreningen Fransk Konst, Auguste Renoir e utstallning*, 1921, no. 51; Stockholm, Liljevachs Konstall, *Frank Konst i Svensk privat ago*, 1926, no. 555; New York, Wildenstein & Co., *Renoir*, 1969, no. 12, illustrated in catalogue

Literature
Ragnar Hoppe, *Katalog over Thorsten Laurins samling au malerei och skulptur*, Stockholm, 1936, ill. pl. 246; John Rewald, "Chocquet and Cézanne," *Gazette des Beaux-Arts*, Vol. 74, series 6, July-Aug. 1969, ill. p. 41, fig. 6

John Rewald identified this small canvas as a preparatory study made for the background of the portrait which depicts Mme. Victor Chocquet seated on the balcony of her apartment overlooking the Tuileries Gardens (*Mme Chocquet Reading*, Private Collection). Chocquet, a customs official, had become acquainted with Renoir and Monet by 1875 and was already listed in the catalogue of the Impressionists' second group exhibition (April, 1876) as a lender of their works. By 1899, the year of his death, Chocquet owned fourteen Renoirs.

While the catalogue of the loan exhibition commemorating the fiftieth anniversay of Renoir's death (Wilderstein, 1969) listed the date of this painting as 1874, Rewald's proposal of 1875-76 seems more plausable and is also accepted by Barbara Ehrlich White (*Renoir, His Life, Art and Letters*, New York, 1984, p.60).

Pierre-Auguste Renoir

Gabrielle Lisant
c. 1894-95
Oil on canvas
15 1/2 x 12 1/4 inches (39.4 x 31.1 cms.)

Provenance
Ambroise Vollard, Paris; André Weil, Paris; René Fribourg, New York (1953); Sotheby's, London, *René Fribourg Sale*, June 26, 1963, p. 61, no. 118, illustrated in catalogue; O'Hana Gallery, London, 1963

Literature
Ambroise Vollard, *Tableaux, Pastels et Dessins de Pierre-Auguste Renoir*, Paris, 1918, Vol. II, p. 129, upper right

When Jean Renoir, the painter's second son was born in September, 1894, Gabrielle Renard, his wife's cousin, came to Paris to be the child's nursemaid. If the proposed date of 1894-95 is correct, Gabrielle would have been about fifteen years old and this would be among the earliest of the many oils Renoir painted using her as a model. It can be compared with *Gabrielle with Necklace* c. 1894 in the Kunstmuseum, Basel.

Claude Monet
(French, 1840-1926)

Le Matin au Bord de la Mer,
1881
Signed Claude Monet and dated lower right
Oil on canvas
23 1/2 x 37 7/8 inches (61 x 81 cms.)

26

Provenance
Galerie Durand-Ruel, Paris (purchased from the artist in May 1881); Potter Palmer, Chicago (1893-1944); Parke-Bernet, New York, Sale, March 16, 1944, lot 73; Durand-Ruel Galleries, New York (puchased at Palmer sale); Sam Salz, Inc., New York; Albert J. Dreitzer, San Francisco, c. 1957-1985; Sotheby's New York, Sale, November 13, 1985, lot 15

Exhibitions
Paris, 251 Rue Saint Honoré, *Exhibition des Artistes Indépendants* (7th Impressionist Exhibition), 1882, no. 83; New York, National Academy of Design, *Celebrated Paintings*, 1887, no. 152; Saint Louis City Art Museum and The Minneapolis Institute of Arts, *Claude Monet*, 1957, no. 51, illustrated in catalogue

Literature
J.-K. Huysmans *Oeuvres Complètes*, VII, Paris, 1929, p. 292; Daniel Wildenstein, *Claude Monet: Biographie et catalogue raisonné*, vol.I, Lausanne and Paris, 1974, no. 651, ill. p.394; Charles Moffett et al, *The New Painting, Impressionism 1874-1886*, exhibition catalogue, Fine Arts Museums of San Francisco and National Gallery of Art, Washington, D.C. 1986, pp.394-95

During the winter of 1880-81, Monet resumed his business relationship with Paul Durand-Ruel. In a letter to him, dated March 8, 1881, the painter announced his intention of leaving for Fécamp on the coast of Normandy where he planned to spend about three weeks working on seascapes. Although Monet had produced numerous views of the beaches and cliffs of his native Normandy in the 1860s, these canvases of Fécamp, Grainval and the beach at Les Petites-Dalles announced a new direction and new formal priorities as the artist explored unusual vantage points and dazzling new color harmonies.

This painting was exhibited with ten other coastal views in the Impressionist Group Show of 1882. The reaction to the works was generally enthusiastic and the novelist and critic Joris-Karl Huysmans called them "the truest seascapes I have ever seen." (Huysmans, *Oeuvres Complètes*, VII, I, p. 292)

In his discussion of the significance of the Normandy seascapes in the catalogue of the 1986 exhibition *The New Painting, Impressionism 1874-1886*, Joel Isaacson calls them "Monet's most advanced work." (p. 386)

Vincent Van Gogh
(Dutch, 1853-1890)

Le Moulin à L'eau (The Watermill at Coll),
1884
Oil on canvas on board
22 3/4 x 31 1/2 inches (51.5 x 78 cms.)

Provenance
Carpenter Schrauer, Breda, November 1885; Brothers M. & J. C. Couvreur, Breda, c. 1900; C. Mouwen, Jr., Breda till 1904; F. Muller & Co., Amsterdam, Sale, May 3, 1904, no. 2 (not sold); Oldenzeel Art Gallery, Rotterdam; Unger and Van Mens, Rotterdam; Private Collection, The Netherlands; Mak Van Waay, Amsterdam, Sale, April 25, 1966, no. 41 *(Brabantse Watermoelen);* Parke-Bernet, New York, Sale 2540, April 16, 1967, lot 18

Exhibitions
's-Hertogenbosch, Noordbrabants Museum, *Van Gogh in Brabant*, November 2, 1987-January 10, 1988, no. 77, illustrated in catalogue

Literature
R. Jacobson, *Onze Kunst*, Amsterdam, 1903, part I, p. 115; Frederick Muller & Cie, *Mouwen Collection Sale. Vincent Van Gogh*, Amsterdam, May 3, 1904, no. 2 *(Le Moulin a l'Eau).* Walther Vanbeselaere, *De Hollandische periode (1880-1885) in het werk van Vincent Van Gogh*, Amsterdam and Antwerp, 1937, pp. 284, 330, 414; Marc Edo Tralbaut, "In Van Gogh's voetspoor te Antwerpen", *De Toerist*, XXXIV, pp. 9, 11, 1955, 360-71; *The Complete Letters of Vincent Van Gogh.* edited by J. Van Gogh-Bonger, New York, 1958, Vol. III, p. 409, LR 50; Annet Tellegen, *Museum Journaal*, February 13, 1968, 117-120, ill. p. 120; Marc Edo Tralbaut, *Vincent Van Gogh*, New York, p. 137, 1969; J.B. De La Faille, *The Works of Vincent Van Gogh*, Amsterdam, 1970, no.48a, p. 61, ill. p.92; *Twenty Five Great Masters of Modern Art: Van Gogh*, Vol. 11, Tokyo, 1980, pl. 4; Jan Hulsker, *The Complete Van Gogh*, New York, 1980, no. 488, pp. 114, 118; Maureen S. Trappeniers, M. Op de Coul et. al., *Van Gogh in*

Brabant, exhibition catalogue, Noordbrabants Museum, 's-Hertogenbosch, 1987, no. 77, pp. 95,209-210

In December 1883, Van Gogh left Drenthe in northern Holland where he had been working for about three months and went to live with his family in the parsonage in Nuenen, Brabant. Despite conflicts with his father, he set up a makeshift studio in a laundry shed behind the house and began to appreciate the landscape and make friendships with the local inhabitants. His interest in peasant life and labor, already informed by his appreciation of the works of J.F. Millet, found new stimulation in this rural environment.

In a letter to his friend, the painter Anthon van Rappard, who had spent ten days with him in Nuenen during May, 1884, Van Gogh provided a description of a painting in progress:

"Since your departure I have been working on a watermill—the one I inquired about in that little bar near the station... It is the same motif as the other two watermills we went to look at together, but this one has two red roofs, and you see it right from the front—with poplars round it. In autumn it will be superb." (*Letters*, LR. 50)

In 1955, on the basis of comparison with extant watermills Marc Edo Tralbaut identified that painting as the *Watermill at Coll*, a village near the station of Eeneind referred to in the letter. The mill, which is about a half-hour's walk from the station, still survives. In 1968, Annet Tellegen redated the letter and the painting from November to the end of May, 1884.

Of *Watermill at Coll*, Hulsker has written "In color and composition it is an exceptionally fine painting, much superior to the other mills done in the fall." (p. 118) The sturdy and sure composition is enlivened by warm hues that testify to the effect of Van Gogh's intense study of color theory—a study to which he refers in his contemporaneous letters.

Camille Pissarro
(French, 1830-1903)

Le Grand Noyer A Eragny
1892
Signed C. Pissarro and dated lower left
Oil on canvas
24 x 29 inches (60 x 73 cms.)

Provenance
Durand-Ruel et Cie, Paris; Marlborough Fine Art Ltd., London; Findlay Galleries, Chicago; Edmund W. Mudge, Jr., Dallas, Texas; Parke-Bernet, New York, Sale 3102, October 28, 1970, lot 24

Exhibitions
Paris, Galerie Durand-Ruel, *4me Exposition Particulière de C. Pissarro,* March, 1893, no. 35

Literature
L.-R. Pissarro and Lionello Venturi, *Camille Pissarro, Son Art, Son Oeuvre,* Paris, 1939, Vol.I, no. 781, ill. pl. 161

Pissarro moved to Eragny-sur-Epte in April 1884, and the gardens and surrounding landscape were among his favorite subjects in the following decade. Although Pissarro had painted numerous landscapes and scenes of farm labor from the 1870s on, the Eragny pictures of the early 1890s suggest that the artist was reassessing his earlier Impressionist approach after a five year hiatus during which he had embraced the theories and techniques of Neo-Impressionism.

Stylistically, the Eragny landscapes are characterized by more luminous and distinctive color harmonies and by more heavily worked pigment. The particularly vibrant palette and almost relief-like surface of this view of a giant walnut tree attest to Pissarro's consumate skill in translating the effects of light in nature into eloquent lyrical statements.

Camille Pissarro

Study For Les Laveuses
c. 1901?
Signed with initials C.P. lower right
Pastel on paper
17 x 9 inches (43.2 x 22.9 cms.)

32

Provenance
Ira Haupt, New York; Parke-Bernet, New York, Sale 2344, April 14, 1965, lot 2

Literature
Pissarro and Venturi, *op. cit.*, Vol. I, no. 1206, p. 248; Vol.II, no. 1206, pl 237.

    This pastel seems to have been made in connection with the painting *Les Laveuses, Etude à Eragny* (Pissarro and Venturi, no. 1206) dated c. 1901. The figure appears in the upper right quadrant of the composition. Carla Gottlieb also linked it with a watercolor in the Boymans-van Beuningen Museum (H.R. Hoetink, *Franse tekeningen uit de 19e eeuw, catalogus Boymans-van Beuningen Museum*, Rotterdam, 1967, no. 209, ill.)

Camille Pissarro

A Macon
c. 1898
Signed C. Pissarro and inscribed Macon lower right
Pencil and watercolor
6 1/2 x 9 1/4 inches (16.5 x 23.5 cms.)

Provenance
Michael Zagayski, Palm Beach; Parke-Bernet, New York, Sale
2635, October 13, 1967, lot 5

Janine Bailly-Herzberg's chronology in the Pissarro exhibition catalogue (Hayward Gallery, London, 30 October, 1980-1 January, 1981; Grand Palais, Paris, 30 January-27 April, 1981; Museum of Fine Arts, Boston, 19 May-9 August, 1981) states that the artist made short trips in June and July of 1898 to Troyes, Chatillon-sur-Seine, Dijon, Macon, Lyons, and Cluny, suggesting that this inscribed watercolor is a souvenir of one of those journeys.

Edgar Germain Hilaire Degas
(French, 1834-1917)

Deux Danseuses en Rose, Les Bras Levés
c. 1900
Signed Degas lower left
Pastel on paper
36 x 19 inches (93 x 50 cms.)

Provenance
Durand-Ruel, Paris, 1918 (bought at the *Vente Atelier Degas*, December 11); Durand-Ruel, New York, 1920; Jean d'Alayer, Paris; O'Hana Gallery, London, 1965

Exhibitions
New York, Durand-Ruel, *Exhibition of Pastels and Drawings by Degas (1834-1917)*, March 11-27, 1920, no. 4; London, O'Hana Gallery, *Summer Exhibition, French Paintings and Sculpture of the Nineteenth and Twentieth Centuries*, May 18-September 17, 1966, no. 11 *(Danseuses en Tutus Roses* 1890), illustrated in catalogue

Literature
Vente Atelier Degas, Paris, 1918, vol.II, p. 108, no. 205; P.A. Lemoisne, *Degas et son Oeuvre*, Paris, 1946-49, vol.III, no. 1390, p. 804; Lilian Browse, *Degas Dancers*, London, 1949, p. 405

Degas's fascination with dance endured for half a century, from the early 1860s through the arrival in Paris of Sergei Diaghelev and the famed *Ballets Russes* in 1909. Ranging from studies of practice and rehearsal to actual performances, his paintings, drawings, and pastels constitute a total record of the dancer's life and testify to the artist's abiding fascination with disciplined physical movement.

After the 1880s, the worsening of his vision inclined Degas to utilize the medium of pastel with greater frequency. Uniting color and drawings, he produced some of his boldest and most simplified designs. Lilian Browse compares this pastel with another work of about 1900, *Deux Danseuses en Corsages, Violets aux Bras Levés* (Lemoisne, no. 1389), formerly in the Heydt Collection, Ascona.

In these late works, Degas usually stressed the rough grain of the pastel and often added touches of charcoal so that he achieved a sense of monumentality and physicality not previously associated with the medium.

38

Jean-Louis Forain
(French, 1852-1931)

La Confidence dans les Coulisses, (L'Aveu)
after 1900
Signed forain lower right
Pastel and watercolor on paper
16 x 12 inches (40.6 x 30.5 cms.)

Provenance
Hirschl & Adler, New York

Exhibitions
New York, Hirschl & Adler, *Jean-Louis Forain, 1852-1931*, March 7-April 1, 1967, no. 43 *(La Confidence dans les Coulisses)*, illustrated in catalogue

Literature
Pictures on Exhibit, Vol. XXX, March 1967, p. 12 *(La Confidence)*

Forain had come into the orbit of Impressionism through his friendship with Degas. Like the latter, he was attracted to the social themes proclaimed in the novels of such contemporaneous naturalist writers as Emile Zola and J.-K. Huysmans.

In her unpublished notes on this pastel, Carla Gottlieb pointed out its similarity to a lithograph *L'Aveu* reproduced in Marcel Guérin's *J.L. Forain, Lithographe*, Paris, 1910 and to an oil *Dans les Coulisses*, c. 1910, formerly in the Durand-Ruel Collection (Durand-Ruel, *19th and 20th Century French Paintings*, New York, 1948, no. 2, pl. XIV). Forain's predilection for scenes of dancers and their predatory "protectors" is well documented in his oeuvre. Yet another oil, *Danseuses et Financier*, c. 1907 Chapellier Collection, Versailles, shows two similar dancers with what appears to be the same male figure as the one depicted in this pastel.

It should be noted that the encounter does not take place in the wings (coulisses), but rather in a dressing room, therefore casting some doubt on the accuracy of the title.

Jean-François Raffaelli
(French, 1850-1924)

Les Maisons au Soleil
Signed J.F. Raffaelli lower left
Oil on board
25 1/2 x 34 inches (65 x 86.5 cms.)

40

Provenance
H. Fürstenberg, Berlin; Sotheby's New York, Sale, Thursday, October 29, 1987, *Important 19th Century European Paintings, Drawings and Watercolors,* lot 147

Despite the objections of some of his Impressionist colleagues, Degas invited Raffaelli to participate in the fifth and sixth group shows (1880-1881). Like Degas, Raffaelli drew inspiration from the modern urban world and was especially drawn to the impoverished citizens of Paris and its increasingly industrialized suburbs. His work never expresses the mainstream Impressionist interest in brilliant color. Instead, it is characterized by a superb sense of form communicated by the forceful draughtsmanship that is evident in this rare landscape of a sun drenched cluster of houses on a hillside.

Childe Hassam
(American, 1859-1935)

Central Park West at 82nd Street
1894?
Signed Childe Hassam and dated lower left
14 1/4 x 17 inches (36.2 x 43.2 cms.)

Provenance
The Milch Galleries, New York; Schneider-Gabriel, New York;
Private Collection, St. Louis Missouri; Max Safron, New York;
Hirschl & Adler, New York, 1966

The Massachusetts born painter was transformed into an Impressionist during a three year's stay in France (1887-1889). Settling in New York on his return, he painted numerous views of parks, squares, and large thoroughfares that recall the Parisian counterparts Monet and Renoir.

In a letter of November 5, 1986, Kathleen Burnside of Hirschl & Adler indicated that Hassam had done a number of promenade subjects from the mid 1890s through about 1910. The Milch Galleries exhibited a canvas entitled *Central Park West, Winter* in a show of the artist's paintings and watercolors (April 26-May 15, 1943). Because the catalogue was not illustrated and contained no measurements, it is impossible to identify this canvas as the one exhibited. However, the gallery's records contained an old photograph of this painting with the notation "Central Park West by Childe Hassam." Since there are no earlier references to a work called *Central Park West at Eighty Second Street,* it is likely that this was not the painting's original title.

Burnside has located a photograph of a closely related work also listed as *Central Park West* (24 1/4 x 17 1/2, signed and dated in the lower left: Childe Hassam, 1894). This painting was sold in 1924 by M. Knoedler and Company to W.H. Dicks of Chicago, but its present location is unknown. Although its format is vertical and its size is somewhat larger, the composition appears to be the same.

The painting will appear in the *catalogue raisonné* being prepared by Stuart P. Feld and Kathleen M. Burnside.

Paul Gauguin
(French, 1848-1903)

Eve
1898-99
Woodcut printed in black on Japan tissue
Initialed "P.G." upper left and numbered "no.1" lower right
11 x 8 3/8 inches (287 x 212 cms.)

Literature
Marcel Guérin, *L'oeuvre gravé de Gauguin* 2 vols., Paris, 1927, no. 57; Richard S. Field, "Gauguin's Woodcuts, Some Sources and Meanings," *Gauguin and Exotic Art*, Philadelphia Museum of Art, 1969, unpaginated

Gauguin did not explore woodcuts until after his return to Paris from his first voyage to Tahiti (1891-93). Conceived as visual accompaniments to his prose poem *Noa Noa (Fragrance, Fragrance)* the initial woodcuts reflected the artist's desire to evoke a distant and unspoiled society before the incursions of Western civilization. Gauguin was well prepared for his work in this medium, having trained himself by carving furniture, doors, shoes, and other objects in Brittany some years earlier. Attacking the wood blocks with gouges, employing needles and rough sandpaper, experimenting with irregular inking and printing procedure, he aimed at calculatedly "primitive" effects that would open other artists' eyes to the expressive potential of the oldest of the printmaking media.

Field has suggested that a door jamb sculpture from the church at Guimiliau, Brittany, depicting Eve and the serpent, may have been the source for this and other native Eves that Gauguin produced in Tahiti.

A photograph pasted on the *Noa Noa* manuscript, p. 51, reproduces a lost drawing of *Eve with a Hooded Figure*.

Paul Gauguin

Te Atua (Les Dieux)
1898-99
Woodcut printed in black on Japan paper
First of two states
9 1/4 x 8 1/8 inches (236 x 208 mms.)
Edition of 30 or more impressions

Provenance
Hirschl & Adler, New York

Literature
Guérin, no. 60; Field

Paul Gauguin

Te Arii Vahine (Femme de Race Royale)
1898-99
Woodcut printed in black on Japan tissue
Signed "P.G." upper left, inscribed in pencil "No. 13", lower
right
6 x 11 7/8 inches (160 x 304 mms.)
Edition of 30 impressions

Provenance
Hirschl & Adler, New York

Literature
Guérin, no. 62; Libuse Sýkorowá, *Gauguin Woodcuts,* London,
1963, no. 5

    The woodcut repeats the principal image of an eponymous
oil, also known as *Woman with Mangoes,* 1896 in the Pushkin
Museum, Moscow
    The badly damaged woodblock in the National Gallery,
Prague, would appear to be its original matrix (Sýkorowá, no. 5)

Paul Gauguin

Misères Humaines (Souvenir de Bretagne)
c. 1899
Woodcut printed in black on Japan tissue
Initialed lower left "P.G." and numbered "1"
8 1/2 x 11 7/8 inches (218 x 298 mms.)
Edition of 30 impressions

Provenance
Hirschl & Adler, New York

Literature
Guérin no. 69

Once again, Gauguin made use of an earlier image and title, as he relocated the figure of the woman from the zincograph of 1889 (Guérin, no. 5) in a Polynesian setting.

46

Paul Gauguin

Te Atua (Les Dieux)
1898-99
Woodcut printed in black on Japan tissue
Second state
Signed "P.G." and title engraved in a horizontal band traversing at about two-thirds of the print's height. Numbered "15" lower right
9 1/2 x 8 1/4 inches (240 x 210 mms.)

Provenance
Hirschl & Adler, New York

Literature
Guérin, no. 61

Field calls *Te Atua* "the most complex woodcut of the last years," anticipating "Picasso's linocuts, for two states from the *same* block are printed over one another to achieve color separations." Field, unpaginated
The two states of *Te Atua* (Guérin, nos. 60 and 61) were originally pasted together, but were separated at some point.

Note: The sixteen woodcuts in the collection will be included in the catalogue of Gauguin's prints being prepared by E.W. Kornfeld, Bern.

Paul Gauguin

Changement De Résidence
1898-99
Woodcut, First state, printed in brown on Japan paper
Signed lower right Paul Gauguin fecit, also titled *Tahiti* upper right
6 5/16 x 11 13/16 inches (160 x 301 mms.)
Edition of 30 impressions

Provenance
Hirschl & Adler, New York

Literature
Guérin, no. 66

A proof of this print is glued to page 189 of the original manuscript of *Noa-Noa* in the Cabinet de Dessins, Louvre. The painting *Rupé-Rupé*, 1899 in the Pushkin Museum, Moscow is also closely related to the imagery of this print which Field interprets as an allegorical representation of the painter's move to the Marquesas Islands—a move which finally took place in 1901.

Pierre Bonnard
(French, 1867-1947)

Femme A La Lampe (Le Couseuse)
1912
Signed Bonnard lower left
Oil on paper, mounted on canvas
17 1/2 x 23 1/2 inches (47 x 62 cms.)

Provenance
Bernheim-Jeune, Paris, 1912; Art Moderne, Lucerne, 1917; Eugène Laffont, Paris, 1920; Georges Bernheim, Paris; Galerie de l'Elysée, Paris; Aimé Maeght, Paris, 1947; André Meyer, New York, 1950; David Landau, Paris, 1959; Sotheby's, London, Sale, November 25, 1959, no. 65; O'Hana Gallery, London, 1964

Exhibitions
London, O'Hana Gallery, *Summer Exhibition: Paintings and Sculpture of the Nineteenth and Twentieth Century*, June-September 1960, no. 1 (circa 1905); Idem., 1962, no. 1; Idem., 1963, no. 2; Idem., no. 1

Literature
Georges Coquiot, *Bonnard*, Paris, 1922, p. 54 *(Femme cousant)*; François-Joachim Beer et al., *Pierre Bonnard*, Marseilles, 1947, pl. 48, pp. 68,166 *(La Couseuse)*; Thadée Natanson, *Le Bonnard*

que je Propose, Geneva, 1951, fig. 18 *(Femme à la Lampe*, 1899); Heinrich Rumpel, *Bonnard*, Bern, 1952, pl. 10, pp. 14, 15, 17 *(Die Lampe*, 1899); Kunsthaus Zurich, *Sammlung Emil G Bührle*, 1958, p. 146; *Femme à la Lampe*, circa 1905; Adrian Bury, "Round about the Galleries, European Masters," *The Connoisseur*, vol. CXLVI, September 1960, p. 53; Jean and Henri Dauberville, *Bonnard, 1906-1918, Catalogue raisonné de l'oeuvre peint*, Paris, 1968, vol. II, no. 687, ill. p. 255

Bonnard made his official painting debut in the Salon des Indépendants in 1891. Three years earlier, as a student at the Académie Julian, he had been part of a closely knit group which included Paul Sérusier, Maurice Denis, and Paul Ransom. This group formed the nucleus of the self-proclaimed *Nabis* (Hebrew for prophets), one of the most influential art movements in the last years of the nineteenth century.

The term *Intimiste* often has been used to describe the style of the images of bourgeois domesticity painted by Bonnard and his friend and fellow *Nabi*, Edouard Vuillard, images which are characterized by simplified forms, intensified contrasts of light and color, and an emphasis on pictorial surface.

Bonnard first turned to compositions of women or children seated at lamp-lit tables, reading or working, c. 1898 (Dauberville, nos. 176, 177). By 1912, he had completed at least seven paintings related to this theme, of which *Intimité La lampe jaune*, c. 1910 (Dauberville, no. 249) is closest to this canvas.

Edouard Vuillard
(French, 1868-1940)

Portrait of the Comtesse Anne Brâncovan de Noailles
c. 1932-34
Signed E. Vuillard lower right
Distemper on canvas
43 3/4 x 50 1/2 inches (111.3 x 128.7 cms.)

Provenance
Jacques Roussel (inherited from the artist); Sam Salz, New York, c. 1954-56; Mr. and Mrs. William Weintraub, Quogue, New York, after 1956; Parke Bernet, New York, Sale no. 2344, April 14, 1965, lot 70.

Exhibitions
Venice, *XIXa Esposizione Biennale Internazionale d'Arte*, 1934, no. 121; Paris, Galerie Charpentier, *Vuillard*, 1948, no. 92; Basel, Kunsthalle, March 26-May 1, 1949, no. 76; Cleveland Museum of Art, *Edouard Vuillard*, January 26-March 14, 1954, and New York, Museum of Modern Art, April 7-June 6, 1954, no. 127.

Literature
XIXa Esposizione Biennale Internazionale d'Arte, Venice, 1934, 2nd ed., p. 288, no. 121; G.B. "Dans les Galeries: Prestige du Dessin Galerie de la 'Gazette des Beaux-Arts'," *L'Amour de l'Art*, vol. XVI. January 1935, p. 35; Waldemar George, "Vuillard et l'Age Heureux", *Art Vivant*, Vol. 7, no. 221, May 1938, p. 35; Jacques Salomon, *Vuillard, Témoignage*, Paris, 1945, pp. 75-84, ill. p. 77; Claude Roger-Marx, *Vuillard et son temps*, Paris, 1946 pp. 101, 105-106;————, *Vuillard, His Life and Work*, London, 1946; André Chastel, *Vuillard*, Paris, 1946, pp. 94, 98; Claude Roger-Marx, *Vuillard*, Paris 1948, p. 19;————, "Edouard Vuillard: Das Bildnis der Comtesse Anna De Noailles," *Du*, no. 7, July 1949, pp. 12-14, ill. p. 15; Jacques Salomon, *Auprès de Vuillard*, Paris, 1953, p. 101; Andrew C. Ritchie, *Edouard Vuillard*, New York, 1954, p. 104, (oil); Jacques Salomon, "Vuillard Paints a Portrait" *Art News*, Vol. 60, no. 9, January, 1962. pp. 25, 26, 57; Stuart Preston, *Edouard Vuillard*, New York, 1970, p. 156, ill. p. 157

Vuillard painted more than forty portraits after 1920—portraits which not only convey the appearance of their subjects, but which reveal, through their sensitive attention to costume and detail, the intimate habits and character of the *haute bourgeoisie* and aristocracy.

The subject of this portrait was a brilliant and striking woman of Greek, Turkish and Rumanian heritage who married the scion of one of France's most distinguished families. A gifted writer and a dazzling conversationalist, the Comtesse presided over a glittering salon which attracted luminaries of the social and intellectual worlds of early twentieth century Paris.

Vuillard painted the Comtesse, already visibly ravaged by her illness, a year before death at the age of fifty-seven. Because she was accustomed to receiving visitors in her bedroom, the artist depicted her in the midst of an enormous Louis XVI bed, surrounded by a profusion of objects.

As was his custom, Vuillard made countless trips to the Comtesse's apartment in order to accumulate visual information for the portrait which he then executed in his studio. His sitter wearied of the artist's almost clinical obsession with detail. She is reported to have told her maid "For heaven's sake, hide that tube of vaseline, M. Vuillard paints everything he sees." (Salomon, 1945, p. 144)

Dissatisfied with the first version of the portrait (Private Collection, Paris), the painter put it aside. The painting under discussion is the second version which the artist exhibited at the Twenty-First Biennale in Venice in 1934. A charcoal study on canvas for this work is in the Musée National de l'art Moderne, Paris.

This painting will appear in the forthcoming Vuillard *catalogue raisonné* being prepared by Antoine Salomon and Juliet Wilson Bareau.

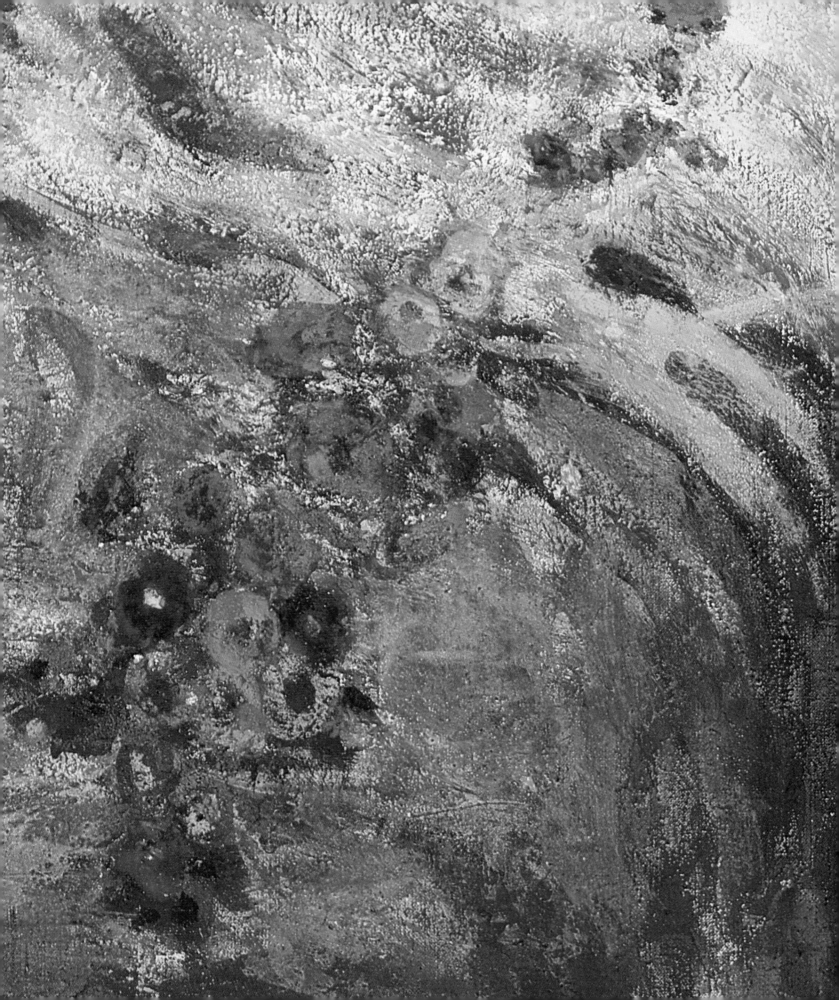

Edouard Vuillard

Counterpane
Study for the *Portrait of the Comtesse de Noailles*
c. 1932.
Atelier stampe "E.V.", lower right
Pastel on paper
9 7/8 x 12 1/2 inches (24 x 31.75 cms)

54

Provenance
Atelier of the Artist; (?) French dealer; Spencer A. Samuels & Co.,
New York, c. 1967.

Exhibitions
(?) Basel, Kusthalle, 1949, (nos. 78-83); New York, Spencer A.
Samuels & Co., *The Intimate Notation*, October-November,
1967, no. 52

Literature
Salomon, 1945, pp. 75-84; Roger-Marx, 1949, pp. 11-15; Salomon,
1962, p. 26, ill. no. 10; Spencer A. Samuels, 1967, p. 33.

Vuillard was so concerned with capturing his sitter's
environment that he produced an unprecedented number of
drawings and pastels of the Comtesse's head, arms and hands, as
well as the flowered bedcover, the table objects, and even the
wallpaper.

This pastel is one of at least six studies made of the floral
motif of the bedcover. Carla Gottlieb, who provided the
documentation for the portrait and this study in 1968, suggested
that it may have been among the pastels shown in the 1949 Basel
exhibition which also included the LeFrak version of the
portrait.

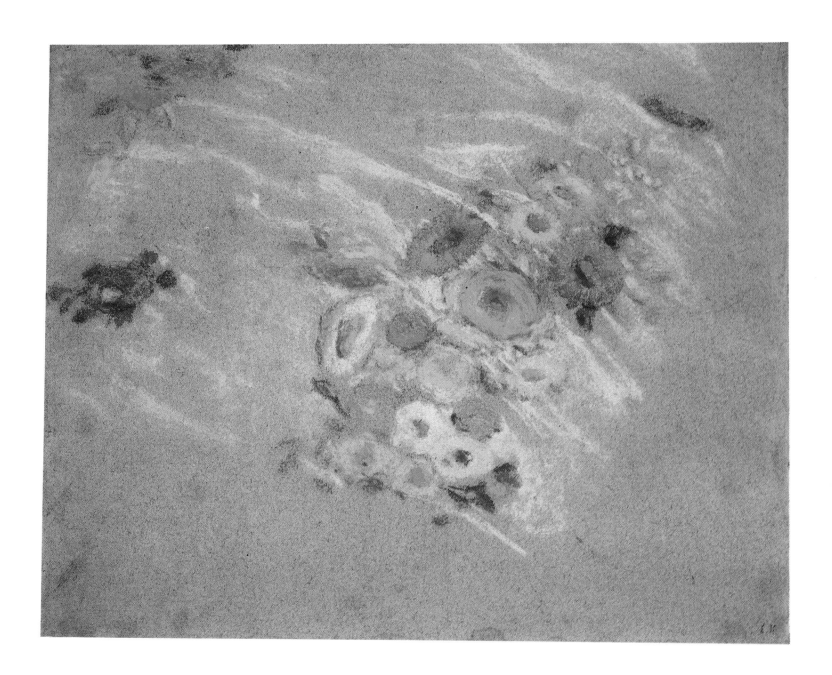

Paul Cézanne
(French, 1839-1906)

Arbres
c. 1890 (Venturi Revised: 1892-94)
Watercolor on paper (probably a page from a sketchbook)
4 1/4 x 7 7/8 inches (12 x 20 cms.)

56

Provenance
Paul Cézanne *fils*, Paris; Sir Kenneth Clark, London; H.J. Bomford, London; George Moos, Geneva; George Waechter, New York; Parke-Bernet, New York, Sale 2635, December 13, 1967, Lot 32.

Literature
Lionello Venturi, *Cézanne, Son Art, Son Oeuvre*, Paris, 1936, Vol. I, "Oeuvres inédites", p. 349; John Rewald, *Paul Cézanne, The Watercolors*, Boston, 1983, no. 356, p. 171, ill. figure 356.

The small scale of this watercolor has persuaded Rewald that it is probably a page from a sketchbook. Like so many of the watercolors of the 1890s the subject is a row of trees, indicated by the most summary washes of blue and green, and its site eludes identification.

Eschewing the use of line, the artist relies entirely on color to define forms and unify the composition. Working from part to part, he relinquishes any notion of compositional hierarchy and emphasizes the immediacy of his senstation as well as its evident incompleteness. Observed individually, the elements do not assume the characteristics of the natural forms which inspired them. They achieve meaning only in their interconnection and, even then, the total image seems more to reflect the painter's concern with the creation of a unifying pattern than with the transcription of visual information.

Georges Rouault
(French 1871-1958)

Les Refugiés
1912
Signed G. Rouault and dated upper right corner.
Watercolor and pastel on paper
11 1/4 x 7 1/2 inches (28.6 x 19 cms.)

58

Provenance
J. Leger & Sons, London; Mary B. Higgins, New York; Spencer
A. Samuel & Co., New York, 1967

Exhibitions
Spencer A. Samuels & Co., New York, *The Intimate Notation*,
October-November 1967, no. 39

Although he exhibited with the Fauves in the Salon
d'Automne from 1905 through 1907, Rouault's subject matter—
the tragedy and dignity of life at the margins of society—and his
predilection for dark colors and oppressive black outlines
isolated him from the mainstream of decorative expressionism.

Working extensively in gouache and watercolor, he frequently
explored the environments of thieves, vagrants and prostitutes.
In this work, he depicted a theme that had been painted some
sixty years earlier by Daumier, an artist he greatly admired.

Raoul Dufy
(French, 1877-1953)

Le Marché Aux Pommes, Quai De L'Hôtel De Ville
1904
Oil on canvas
21 1/4 x 25 inches (53.9 x 63.5 cms.)

Provenance
Vinot, Paris (c. 1953-54); The Lefevre Gallery, London, 1957; Schoneman Galleries, New York, 1959

Exhibitions
Paris, Salon des Indépendants, *20me Exposition*, February 21-March 24, 1904, no. 819, p. 57; Paris, Musée National d'Art Moderne, *Raoul Dufy, 1877-1953*, 1953, no. 8, p. 18; London, The Tate Gallery, *Raoul Dufy*, January 9-February 7, 1954, no. 3; London, The Lefevre Gallery, *XX Century French Masters*, March 1958, no. 7

Literature
Pierre Courthion, *Raoul Dufy*, Geneva, 1951, p. XI, ill., pl. 15; *Raoul Dufy, 1877-1953*, exhibition catalogue; Musée National d'Art Moderne, Paris 1953, p. 18; Keith Sutton, "The Masters Revisited," *Art News & Review*, vol. XI, no. 2, February 14, 1959, p. 8; "Notable Works of Art Now on the Market," *Burlington Magazine*, vol. CI, November 1969, p. XXIII, n.p.; Maurice Laffaille, *Raoul Dufy, catalogue raisonné de l'oeuvre peint*, Geneva, 1976, Tome I, no. 83

In the catalogue of the 1953 Dufy memorial exhibition at the Musée National d'Art Moderne, Bernard Dorival first identified this painting as *Le Quai de l'Hôtel de Ville*, in the Salon des Indépendents of 1904.

This freely-brushed view of the market along the Seine still reflects Dufy's ongoing interest in Impressionist subject matter and technique—an interest that would shortly give way to a preoccupation with intense color and drastically simplified form inspired by his increasing contact with Matisse and his circle.

Raoul Dufy

Promenade Au Bois De Boulogne
1913
Signed Raoul Dufy lower right
Oil on canvas
35 x 45 5/8 inches (89 x 116 cms.)

Provenance
Mme. Raoul Dufy; Robert, Paris; Jean Planque, Paris, 1956;
Mme. Marguerite de la Chapelle, Paris c. 1958; Hirschl & Adler,
New York, 1967

Exhibitions
Paris, Salon des Indépendants, *29me Exposition*, March 19-May
18, 1913, No. 928; Amsterdam, E.J. van Wisselingh & Co.,
Maîtres Francais XIXme et XXme Siècle, November 25-
December 20, 1965, no. 7

Literature
Laffaille, Tome I, no. 381, ill.; Diane Kelder, *The Great Book of
Post-Impressionism*, New York 1986, no. 268, p. 251; ————,
L'heritage de l'Impressionisme, Lausanne, 1986, no. 268, p. 251

After 1908, Dufy began to distance himself from the Fauves.
Working with Braque at L'Estaque, he immersed himself in a
study of Cézanne. Over the next few years, he devoted himself
once again to Parisian themes such as horses and riders in the
Bois de Boulogne, producing compositions which resume
Impressionist themes while introducing simplified structure, a
lighter facture and bright color.

Raoul Dufy

La Modèle Hindoue
1930
Signed Raoul Dufy, dated and inscribed *à Emilienne* lower right
Oil on canvas
16 3/4 x 22 1/2 inches (42.5 x 57 cms.)

Provenance
Dr. A. Roudinesco, New York, (acquired from the artist); Parke-Bernet, New York, Sale 2742, October 10, 1968, lot 23

Exhibitions
Paris, Musée National d'Art Moderne, *Raoul Dufy, 1877-1953*, 1953, no. 58; Paris, Galerie Bernheim-Jeune, *Chefs-d'Oeuvre de Raoul Dufy*, 1959, no. 22

Literature
Laffaille, Tome III, no. 1172, ill.

This canvas was one of a series of eight paintings posed for by the Indian model Anmavati Ponty in Dufy's studio in the Impasse de Guelma in Monmartre between 1928 and 1930. It should be compared with Laffaille, nos. 1171, 1173, 1174, 1175 and 1176.

Dufy became aquainted with the Rumanian-born physician Dr. A. Roudinesco in 1922, and from that time, the latter became one of his principal collectors.

Maurice de Vlaminck
(French, 1876-1958)

Vue de Chatou sur Seine, (Village au Bord d'une Riviere)
c. 1909
Signed Vlaminck lower left
Oil on canvas
25 1/4 x 31 1/2 inches (64.1 x 80 cms.)

Provenance
Leicester Galleries, London, 1937; Mr. and Mrs. Carter C. Higgins, Worcester, Mass., 1938-1967; Parke-Bernet, New York, Sale 2540, April 6, 1967, lot 33

Exhibitions
Boston, Margaret Brown Gallery, *Loan Exhibition: From Two Private Collections*, 1946, no. 7; Worcester Art Museum *Objects of Art Owned in and Near Worcester*, 1950-51 (unnumbered)

Literature
Worcester Art Museum, *News Bulletin and Calendar*, Vol. XVI, no. 3, December 1950, p. 13; Maurice Genevoix, *Vlaminck*, Paris, 1954, p. 14 top

This painting, acquired as *Village au Bord d'une Riviere*, was identified by Carla Gottlieb as a view of Chatou, a popular boating spot on the Seine just west of Paris, which inspired Renoir and other Impressionists to paint numerous light-filled canvases in the 1870s and 80s. Vlaminck had lived in Chatou for a few years before he met and formed a close working relationship there with André Derain in 1900. For a time the two painters shared a studio in an abandoned restaurant which overlooked the bridge that is visible in the painting. Their collaboration was the inception of what Vlaminck later termed "The School of Chatou," a reference to their common interest in intensely colored, heavily impastoed canvases depicting the village and its surrounding landscape.

This canvas was painted a few years after Vlaminck's Fauvist period, when his interest in direct and passionate response to nature was gradually giving way to a new concern with structure inspired by the revelations of Cézanne's landscapes.

A more disciplined approach is already evident in the tightly-knit rectilinear character of this painting's composition and in the relatively subdued palette and the more uniform brushwork the artist employed. In place of Fauvist tension and energy, a new sense of order and monumentality permeate this work.

66

Maurice de Vlaminck

Paysage Près De Chatou,
c. 1909-1910
Signed Vlaminck lower right
Oil on canvas
26 x 32 inches (66 x 81 cms.)

Provenance
Alex Maguy, Paris; O'Hana Gallery, London, 1966

Exhibitions
London, O'Hana Gallery, *Summer Exhibition. French Paintings and Sculpture of the Nineteenth and Twentieth Centuries*, May 18-September 17, 1966, no. 48

After 1907, with Derain more and more inclined to work in the south of France, Vlaminck worked alone at Chatou. He continued to study Cézanne and also gravitated for a time toward the circle of Picasso whose reputation and influence were growing at the expense of Matisse and Fauvism.

Vlaminck painted this view of houses on the outskirts of Chatou in tones that are resonant rather than vivid, using regular brushstrokes that emphasize the nearly geometric character of both architecture and nature.

Maurice de Vlaminck

Nature Morte Aux Artichauts,
c. 1926-28
Signed Vlaminck lower left
Oil on canvas
32 1/2 x 46 inches (82 x 117 cms.)

Provenance
Dr. A Roudinesco, New York (acquired from the artist); Parke-Bernet, New York, Sale 2742, October 10, 1968, lot 20

Exhibitions
Paris, Galerie Bernheim-Jeune, *Retrospective Vlaminck*, 1933, no. 10; Warsaw, National Museum, *De Manet à Nos Jours*, 1937, no. 86; Basel, Kunsthalle, *Vlaminck, Dufy, Rouault*, 1939; Paris, Galerie Charpentier, *Cent Chefs-d'Oeuvres des Peintres de L'Ecole de Paris*, 1946, p. 90, illustrated in catalogue; Rotterdam, Boymans-Van Beuningen Museum, *Quatre siècles de la Nature morte en France*, 1954, no. 137; Paris, Galerie Charpentier, *L'oeuvre de Vlaminck*, 1956, no. 92

Literature
Genevoix, no. 4 ill.

By 1925, Vlaminck had settled permanently at La Tourilliere, outside of Paris, where he found it difficult to adjust to the monotony of the landscape. Perhaps the frustration of painting it induced him to take up still life again. Always directly inspired by his physical surroundings, by simple and familiar things, he began to paint kitchen objects, fruit, vegetables, bottles of wine—the traditional ingredients of the genre.

In *Nature Morte aux Artichauts*, the table objects are really a pretext for an intense study of form and tonal harmony which ultimately transcends their scale and renders them as solemn and monumental as the elements of landscape or architecture.

Kees van Dongen
(Dutch, 1877-1968)

Le Pique-Nique Au Louvard,
c. 1924
Signed Van Dongen, lower left
Oil on Canvas
32 x 39 1/2 inches (81.3 x 100.3 cms.)

Provenance
Dr. A. Roudinesco, New York (acquired from the artist); Parke-Bernet, New York, Sale 2742, October 10, 1968, lot 29

Exhibitions
Paris, Galerie Charpentier, *Plaisirs de la Campagne*, 1954, no. 168, illustrated in catalogue; Paris, Galerie Charpentier, *Cent Tableaux des Collections Privées*, 1960, no. 102

Literature
Edouard des Courieres, *Van Dongen*, Paris, 1925, ill., pl. 60; Roy McMullen, "Van Dongen Remembers", *Réalités*, June 1960, ill., p. 66; Louis Chaumeil, *Van Dongen*, Geneva, 1967, no. 158, ill., p. 210

Van Dongen was already a painter of some reputation when he exhibited two canvases in the celebrated Salon d'Automne of 1905 along with those of Matisse, Marquet, Derain, Vlaminck and other artists who were characterized as Fauves (wild beasts) by the critic Louis Vauxcelles.

Always drawn to provocative and sensual themes, his interest in vibrant and expressive color survived the official life of Fauvism. During the years following the First World War, Van Dongen was extremely fashionable and his financial success permitted a life-style that suited his enormous appetite for pleasure.

Roy McMullen maintains that this canvas depicts one of the many elegant picnics organized by the painter for his worldly Parisian friends at his country estate some sixty kilometers from Paris. The eighteenth century chateau, situated in a large park, forms the backdrop for a sumptuous lunch spread out on rich oriental carpets. "The tall woman in the centre, who is having her hand kissed by a late arrival, is Madam Jasmy who was Van Dongen's companion for nearly twenty years...." (McMullen, p. 66)

Van Dongen's parties were famous for their high spiritedness and there is clearly a suggestion of a modern bacchanal in the foreground of the composition.

Kees Van Dongen

Tête de Femme Tournée de Trois Quarts,
c. 1920
Signed Van Dongen lower left
Oil on canvas
21 3/4 x 18 inches (55.3 x 46 cms.)

74

Provenance
Edgardo Acosta Gallery, Beverly Hills; Elliot and Ruth Handler, Los Angeles; Sotheby's, New York, Sale, November 13, 1985, no. 56, illustrated in catalogue

Exhibitions
Paris, Musée National d'Art Moderne, (?); Rotterdam, Boymans-van Beuningen Museum, *Van Dongen*, 1967-68, no. 108, illustrated in the catalogue

This head seems to date from 1920 or shortly thereafter, a period when the artist executed a number of similarly high-colored canvases depicting heads and torsos of young women.

The years following the end of the First World War in France were marked by unprecedented hedonism, the rejection of social conventions, and in particular, by a form of women's liberation that expressed itself in the emergence of the "garçonne," a young woman who embraced free love, rejected motherhood and affected short hair and men's attitudes.

Van Dongen acknowledged that he had always been drawn to "cocottes et excentriques" and this vividly painted French flapper certainly exemplifies the exaggerated styles and aggressive makeup of the cynical young women of the period.

Wassily Kandinsky
(Russian, 1866-1944)

Kirche In Froschhausen
1908
Signed, titled, numbered AS455 and dated on the reverse
Oil on board
17 3/4 x 13 inches (45 x 33 cms.)

Provenance
Dalzell Hatfield Gallery, Los Angeles; H.F. Stern, Michigan; Nanette Fabray, New York; Parke-Bernet, New York, Sale, May 15, 1963, lot 68; Private Collection; Parke-Bernet, New York, Sale 3102, October 28, 1970, lot 51

Exhibitions
San Francisco, California, Palace of the Legion of Honor, 1961

Literature
Peter Selz, *German Expressionist Painting*, Berkeley, 1957, pp. 182-83, ill.; Will Grohmann, *Wassily Kandinsky, Life and Work*, New York, 1958, no. 580, ill., p. 397

Kandinsky abandoned a promising career as a lawyer in Moscow to study painting in Munich. Initially attracted to the techniques of Impressionism, he spent considerable time in Paris from 1905 through 1907, working and exhibiting at the Salon d'Automne and the Indépendants. His direct experience with Fauvism, while of limited duration, served to catalyze his own search for greater freedom of subject and more expressive color.

This canvas was inspired by a church in Froschhausen near the picturesque village of Murnau in the foothills of the Bavarian Alps. There, Kandinsky and his companion, the painter Gabriele Münter, discovered the folk art technique of *hinterglasmalerei* in peasant houses. These glass paintings, with their heavy lead outlines and brightly colored flat shapes, stimulated Kandinsky to achieve similar effects in his canvases, marking a further stage in his progression toward the use of expressive color and increasingly abstracted form.

Henri Matisse
(French, 1869-1954)

Femme Avec Anemones,
c. 1920
Signed Henri Matisse lower right
Oil on canvas
13 1/4 x 22 inches (33.5 x 55.5 cms.)

Provenance
Galerie Bernheim-Jeune, Paris; Reinhardt Gallery, New York; Frank Crowninshield, New York; Parke-Bernet, New York, Sale October 20, 21, 1943, lot 78; J.B. Neumann, New York, 1945; Helen Adams Bobbs, Indianapolis; Parke-Bernet, New York, Sale 3102, October 28, 9970, lot 35

Exhibitions
New York, Museum of Modern Art, 1940; Lincoln, Nebraska, Nebraska Art Association, *56th Annual Exhibition of Contemporary Art*, 1946, no. 177; Indianapolis, John Herron Art Museum, *European Masters in Indiana Homes*, 1952, no. 45

Literature
"Matisse," *Cahiers d'Aujourd'hui*, Paris, 1920,ill. 38; Adolphe Basler, *Henri Matisse*, Leipzig, 1924, pl. 23; Encyclopedia Britannica, 1929, (14th Ed), Vol. XVII, illlus. pl. XX; Mario Luzi and Massimo Carra, *L'Opera di Matisse della rivolta 'fauve' all'intimismo, 1904-1928*, Milan, 1971, no. 321, ill.; Pierre Schneider and Massimo Carra, *Tout l'oeuvre peint de Matisse, 1904-1928*, Paris, 1982, no. 321, ill.

From 1918, Nice became the critical locus for Matisse's work, stimulating a major shift in content and style. Color and light invaded the Nice canvases which exude an aura of sensuousness and repose that prompted attacks from critics more accustomed to the problematic formalism of Cubist painting.

A letter from the artist's daughter, Marguerite Duthuit, to David Nash of Parke-Bernet (October 6, 1970) states that this canvas was executed in Nice in 1920. It is closely related to a group of paintings done in Matisse's studio in the Hôtel Mediterraneé: *Le peintre et son modèle, intérieur d'Atelier*, 1919 in the collection of Mr. and Mrs. Donald B. Marron, New York, *La Meditation-Après le Bain*, 1920 in a private collection, and *Le Petit-Déjeuner*, 1920 in the Philadelphia Museum of Art.

The model has been identified as Antoinette, who worked for Matisse until about September 1920, suggesting that the painting was done earlier that year.

78

Maurice Utrillo
(French, 1883-1955)

Tabac—Restaurant, Montmartre (Street Scene Montmartre)
1932
Signed Maurice Utrillo V(aladon) and dated lower right
Oil on canvas
20 1/2 x 24 3/4 inches (52 x 62.9 cms.)

Provenance
Paul Petrides (acquired from the artist); Jacques Zucker, Paris;
Schoneman Galleries, New York, 1960

The illegitimate son of Suzan Valadon, a painter who had served as a model for Renoir, Utrillo received lessons from his mother and also studied the works of Sisley and Pissarro. An habitue of cafes in Montmartre, he initially sold his work to local patrons and dealers, but by 1912, he began to attract wider attention and his reputation grew steadily.

Despite life-long bouts with alcoholism and mental illness, Utrillo was extraordinarily prolific. He often used ordinary postcard views as a source of inspiration and his paintings project a timeless simplicity and directness that appealed to a public weary of the complex aesthetic issues that had dominated the Parisian avant-garde for nearly half a century.

82

Marc (

(French,

Le Violi
c. 1930
Signed (
Gouache
19 3/4 x

Provena
Helen S
1948/9-(
lot 40

Exhibit
New Yo
Ceremo
Zagaysk

Literatu
Lionello
Charles
Marc C

Cha
in asce
structur
dent vi
fragmer
convey
Russia
This
a house
emigrés
Megève
contact:
may ha
images
permea
charact

Pablo Picasso

(Spanish, 1881-1973)

Le Déjeuner Sur L'Herbe No. 2,
February 28, 1960
Signed Picasso lower left, dated on the reverse
Oil on canvas
44 1/2 x 57 1/8 inches (113 x 144.8 cms.)

Provenance
Galerie Louise Leiris, Paris, 1962 (acquired from the artist);
Galerie Berggruen, Paris, 1962; O'Hana Gallery, London, 1966

Exhibitions
Paris, Galerie Louise Leiris, *Picasso. Les Déjeuners sur l'Herbe
1960-61*, June 6-July 13, 1962, no. 2

Literature
Douglas Cooper, *Picasso, Les Déjeuners sur l'Herbe 1960-1961*,
Paris, 1962, no. 2; *Idem.* 1963, pl. 5, p. 12; John Richardson,
"Picasso at Eighty-Five," *Art and Artists*, Vol. II, no. 4, July
1967, p. 31; Christian Zervos, *Pablo Picasso*, Vol. 19, *oeuvres de
1959 a 1961*, Paris, 1968, no. 201, pl. 54

Picasso had done fifteen variations on Delacroix's *Les
femmes d'Alger* (1954-55) and forty-five variations on Velasquez's
Las Meniñas (1957) before he embarked on the first line
drawings related to the *Déjeuner sur l'Herbe* series on August 10,
1959. While Manet's once controversial masterpiece offered him
yet another opportunity to raid the past, it also provided a
specific vehicle for the recapitulation of themes dear to him—the
artist's model, bathers, the female monster, and bucolic pleasure.
Moreover, it enabled him to establish yet another living
relationship between his own art and the great art of the past.
Picasso eventually produced twenty-seven painted variations
on this theme between February 17, 1960 and August 19, 1961. Of
the four ink drawings which mark the inception of the series in
the previous year, no. IV(Cooper, pl. 6) is closest to this version.

Marc Chagall

La Mariée et Le Groom, (Le Couple à la Fenêtre),
1949
Signed Chagall lower right
Gouache and india ink on buff paper
25 1/2 x 19 1/4 inches (64.8 x 48.9 cms.)

Provenance
Herman E. Cooper, New York, 1958; Parke-Bernet, New York, Sale 2540, April 6, 1967, lot 46

Exhibitions
Tokyo, National Museum of Western Art *Exposition Marc Chagall*, October 1-November 10, 1963, no. 168 *(La Fiançée et le Groom)* p. 113 and Kyoto Municipal Museum, November 20-December 10, 1963; New York, Marlborough-Gerson Galleries, *Modern Masters Drawings and Watercolors*, 1966, no. 27 *(Bride and Groom)*, illustrated in catalogue

Literature
Franz Meyer, *Marc Chagall*, New York, 1963, no. 789, as *Le Couple à la Fenêtre*

The imagery of Chagall's oeuvre is permeated with reminiscences of Bella, his beloved fiancée and bride. After her death in 1944, the familiar repertory of motifs—the floating couple, flowers, fruits, birds, and windows—is deployed with a muted tonality that imbues it with a new, lyric melancholy.

Marc Chagall

La Trapeziste Rouge,
c. 1950
Signed Chagall lower left
Wash, pastel and ink on paper
19 x 18 inches (48.3 x 45.7 cms.)

Provenance
Galerie Maeght, Paris, 1957; J. Goldschmidt, Paris; Schoneman Galleries, New York, 1956

The circus had inspired some of Chagall's most ebullient canvases in the 1930s, and it would provide the point of departure for numerous works in an unprecedented variety of media from 1950 until his death. In this pastel, the vibrant red color and the calligraphic economcy of the drawing project the energy of the performer and of her environment with a palpable sense of immediacy.

Pablo Picasso
(Spanish, 1881-1973)

Le Déjeuner Sur L'Herbe No. 2,
February 28, 1960
Signed Picasso lower left, dated on the reverse
Oil on canvas
44 1/2 x 57 1/8 inches (113 x 144.8 cms.)

Provenance
Galerie Louise Leiris, Paris, 1962 (acquired from the artist);
Galerie Berggruen, Paris, 1962; O'Hana Gallery, London, 1966

Exhibitions
Paris, Galerie Louise Leiris, *Picasso. Les Déjeuners sur l'Herbe
1960-61,* June 6-July 13, 1962, no. 2

Literature
Douglas Cooper, *Picasso, Les Déjeuners sur l'Herbe 1960-1961,*
Paris, 1962, no. 2; *Idem.* 1963, pl. 5, p. 12; John Richardson,
"Picasso at Eighty-Five," *Art and Artists,* Vol. II, no. 4, July
1967, p. 31; Christian Zervos, *Pablo Picasso,* Vol. 19, *oeuvres de
1959 a 1961,* Paris, 1968, no. 201, pl. 54

Picasso had done fifteen variations on Delacroix's *Les
femmes d'Alger* (1954-55) and forty-five variations on Velasquez's
Las Meniñas (1957) before he embarked on the first line
drawings related to the *Déjeuner sur l'Herbe* series on August 10,
1959. While Manet's once controversial masterpiece offered him
yet another opportunity to raid the past, it also provided a
specific vehicle for the recapitulation of themes dear to him—the
artist's model, bathers, the female monster, and bucolic pleasure.
Moreover, it enabled him to establish yet another living
relationship between his own art and the great art of the past.

Picasso eventually produced twenty-seven painted variations
on this theme between February 17, 1960 and August 19, 1961. Of
the four ink drawings which mark the inception of the series in
the previous year, no. IV(Cooper, pl. 6) is closest to this version.

Pablo Picasso

Funambule,
1970
Signed Picasso and dated 1/6/1970 II lower right
Colored pencil and colored ink on paper
12 x 8 1/2 inches (30.8 x 22.8 cms.)

Provenance
Galerie Louise Leiris (acquired from the artist); O'Hana
Gallery, London

Literature
Zervos, *Pablo Picasso*, vol. 32, *oeuvres de 1970*, Paris, 1977, no.
107, p. 43

Pablo Picasso

Tête de Femme.
1970
Signed Picasso and dated 21.7.70 upper left
Colored pencil and colored ink on paper
12 5/8 x 9 3/4 inches (32.3 x 25 cms.)

Provenance
Galerie Louise Leiris, Paris (acquired from the artist); O'Hana
Gallery, London

Literature
Zervos, vol. 32, no. 235, p. 76

Pablo Picasso

Le Peintre et Son Modèle, March 3, 4, 1963, no. 1
1963
Signed Picasso lower left
Oil on canvas
20 x 42 1/2 inches (50 x 107 cms.)

Provenance
Galerie Louise Leiris, Paris, 1964; Schoneman Galleries, New York, 1964

Exhibitions
Paris, Galerie Louise Leiris, *Picasso: Peintures 1962-1963*, January 15-February 15, 1964, no. 21, illustrated in catalogue

Literature
Helène Parmelin, *Picasso, the Artist and His Model*, New York, 1965, p. 6, ill. p. 22; Christian Zervos, *Pablo Picasso*, vol. 23, *oeuvres de 1962 et 1963*, Paris, 1971, vol. 23, no. 158, p. 78

This time-worn subject continued to provide inspiration for such modern masters as Matisse and Picasso who adopted it for some of their most profound discourses on the art of painting. Beginning work on February 22, 1963, Picasso proceeded at a frenzied pace. On March 2 alone, he painted four canvases and the green configuration of the model in this version had already emerged. By the time he relinquished the subject in mid-June, he had done some sixty works which vary greatly in scale and imagery.